GURREN LAGANN

ART WORKS

CRIMSON LOTUS / SPIRAL STONE

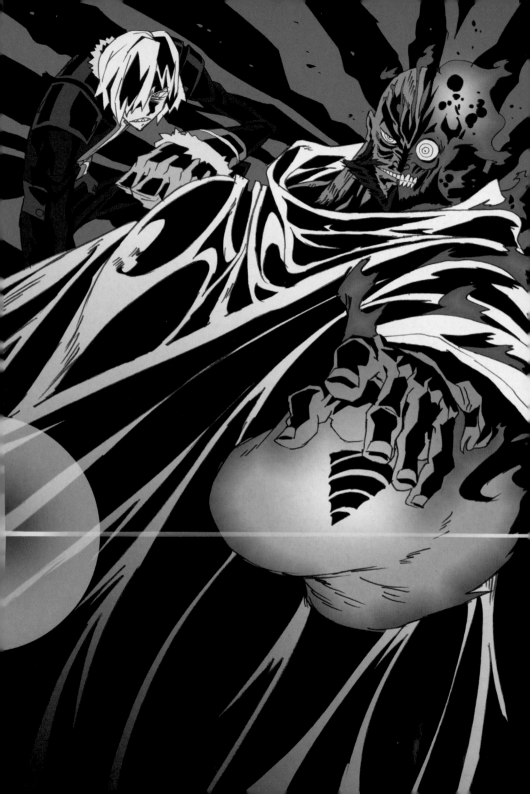

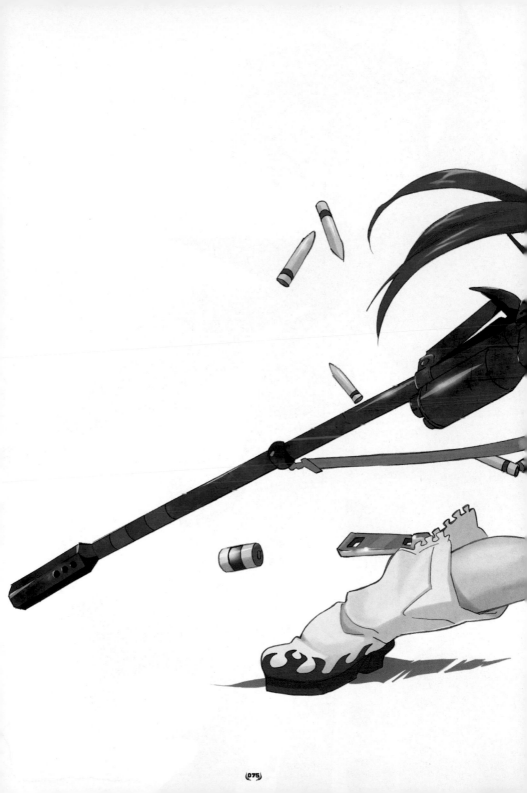

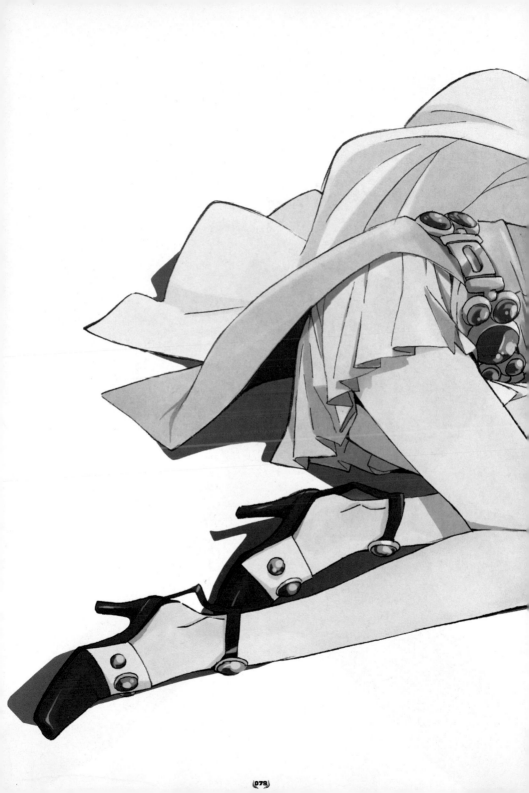

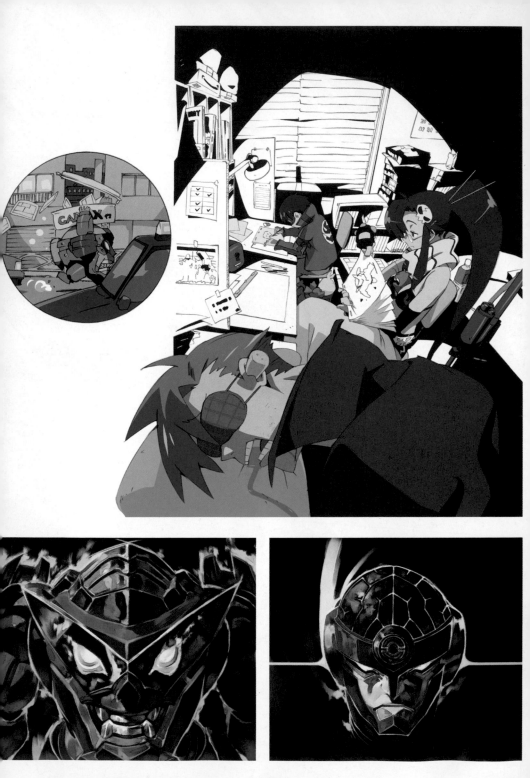

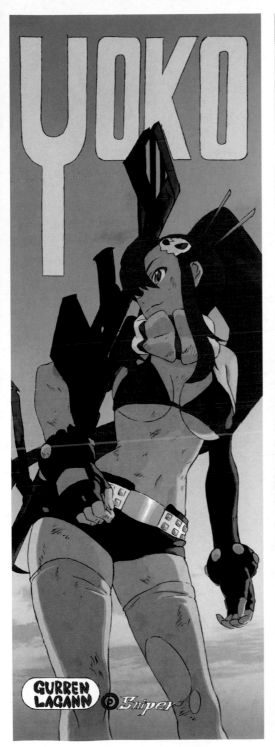

YOKO

KAMINA

GURREN LAGANN ©Sniper

SPACE
ViRAL

GURREN★LAGANN

GURREN LAGANN

SIMON

KING

KITTAN

LAZENGANN

NIA

Bang!!

ILLUSTRATIONS INDEX

ILLUSTRATIONS INDEX

P-018
Base Art:
ATSUSHI NISHIGORI
Finish: SANOKUMI
SFX:
FUMIHIKO MOROHASHI

Debut:
TOKUMA SHOTEN
"ANIMAGE MONTHLY"
FEBRUARY 2007 ISSUE

P-020
Illustration: SUSHIO

Debut:
TOKUMA SHOTEN
"ANIMAGE MONTHLY"
MAY 2007 ISSUE

P-022
Illustration: SUSHIO

Finish:
SUSHIO / SANOKUMI

Debut:
TOKUMA SHOTEN
"ANIMAGE MONTHLY"
JUNE 2007 ISSUE

P-024
Base Art:
CHIKASHI KUBOTAA
Finish: SANOKUMI
SFX: CHIKASHI KUBOTA

Debut:
TOKUMA SHOTEN
"ANIMAGE MONTHLY"
SEPTEMBER 2007 ISSUE

P-025
Base Art:
CHIKASHI KUBOTA
Finish: SANOKUMI
SFX: CHIKASHI KUBOTA

Debut:
TOKUMA SHOTEN "ANIMAGE
MONTHLY" SEPTEMBER 2007 ISSUE

P-026
Base Art:
YAMATO KOJIMA
Finish: SANOKUMI
SFX: HIROMI WAKABAYASHI

Debut:
TOKUMA SHOTEN "ANIMAGE
MONTHLY" APRIL 2007 ISSUE
BONUS CONTENT

P-026
Base Art:
MASAKI YAMADA

Finish:
NORIKO MASHIKO

Debut:
GAKUSHU KENKYUSHA
"ANIMEDIA MONTHLY"
SEPTEMBER 2007 ISSUE

P-009
Base Art:
YUKA SHIBATA
Finish: SANOKUMI
SFX: BIHOU

Debut:
KADOKAWA SHOTEN
"NEWTYPE MONTHLY"
JULY 2007 ISSUE

P-010
Illustration:
SUSHIO

Debut:
KADOKAWA SHOTEN
"NEWTYPE MONTHLY"
MAY 2007 ISSUE

P-012
Base Art:
HITOMI HASEGAWA
Finish: SANOKUMI
BG: JUN TAMAYA

Debut:
KADOKAWA SHOTEN
"NEWTYPE MONTHLY"
SEPTEMBER 2007 ISSUE

P-014
Base Art:
KOUICHI MOTOMURA
Finish: SANOKUMI
BG: BIHOU

Debut:
KADOKAWA SHOTEN
"NEWTYPE MONTHLY"
OCTOBER 2007 ISSUE

P-016
Base Art:
KIKUKO SADAKATA
Finish: SANOKUMI

Debut:
KADOKAWA SHOTEN "NEW-
TYPE MONTHLY FEBRUARY
ISSUE BONUS NEWTYPE
ROMANCE" WINTER 2007

P-017
Base Art:
KATSUZOU HIRATA
Finish: SANOKUMI

Debut:
KADOKAWA SHOTEN
"NEWTYPE MONTHLY
APRIL ISSUE BONUS
NEWTYPE ROMANCE"
SPRING 2007

P-017
Base Art:
KIKUKO SADAKATA
Finish: SANOKUMI

Debut:
KADOKAWA SHOTEN
"NEWTYPE MONTHLY
NOVEMBER ISSUE
BONUS NEWTYPE
ROMANCE" AUTUMN 2007

COVER
Base Art:
ATSUSHI NISHIGORI
Finish: SANOKUMI
SFX: ATSUSHI NISHIGORI
BG: BIHOU

Debut: EXCLUSIVE ART
FOR THIS BOOK

P-002
Layout: HIROYUKI IMAISHI
Base Art:
ATSUSHI NISHIGORI /
YOU YOSHINARI
Finish: SANOKUMI
SFX: DAISUKE KIKUCHI
Debut: MAIN VISUAL
FOR TV SERIES

P-003
Base Art:
ATSUSHI NISHIGORI
Finish: SANOKUMI
SFX:
ATSUSHI NISHIGORI
Debut: MAIN VISUAL
FOR TV SERIES

P-004
Base Art:
ATSUSHI NISHIGORI
Finish: SANOKUMI
BG: DAISUKE KIKUCHI

Debut:
KADOKAWA SHOTEN
"NEWTYPE MONTHLY"
SEPTEMBER 2006 ISSUE

P-006
Base Art:
KOUICHI MOTOMURA
Finish: SANOKUMI
BG: BIHOU

Debut:
KADOKAWA SHOTEN
"NEWTYPE MONTHLY"
JANUARY 2007 ISSUE

P-008
Base Art:
ATSUSHI NISHIGORI
Finish: SANOKUMI
SFX: ATSUSHI NISHIGORI

Debut:
KADOKAWA SHOTEN
"NEWTYPE MONTHLY"
OCTOBER 2006 ISSUE

P-009
Base Art:
CHIKASHI KUBOTA
Finish: SANOKUMI
SFX: CHIKASHI KUBOTA

Debut:
KADOKAWA SHOTEN
"NEWTYPE MONTHLY"
APRIL 2007 ISSUE

P-038

Illustration:
HIROKI SHINAGAWA

Debut:
GAINAX NET
"ALTERNATE VISIONS"
ROUND 4

P-036

Base Art:
SHINGO ABE

Finish: SANOKUMI

Debut:
KODANSHA
"TV MAGAZINE"
JULY 2007 ISSUE

P-027

Base Art:
ATSUSHI NISHIGORI

Finish: SANOKUMI

SFX: ATSUSHI NISHIGORI

Debut:
HOBBY JAPAN "HOBBY
JAPAN MONTHLY"
MAY 2007 ISSUE

P-039

Illustration:
HIROKI SHINAGAWA

Debut:
GAINAX NET
"ALTERNATE VISIONS"
ROUND 4

P-036

Illustration:
DAISUKE SUZUKI
(SANJIGEN)

Debut:
KODANSHA
"TV MAGAZINE"
OCTOBER 2007 ISSUE

P-027

Base Art:
KAZUHIRO TAKAMURA

Finish: SANOKUMI

SFX: KAZUHIRO TAKAMURA

BG: BIHOU

Debut:
GAKUSHU KENKYUSHA
"MEGAMI MAGAZINE"
JULY 2007 ISSUE (VOL.86)

P-039

Illustration:
HIROKI SHINAGAWA

Debut:
GAINAX NET
"ALTERNATE VISIONS"
ROUND 5

P-037

Illustration:
HIROKI SHINAGAWA

Debut:
GAINAX NET
"ALTERNATE VISIONS"
ROUND 1

P-028

Base Art:
SATOSHI YAMAGUCHI

Finish: SANOKUMI

BG:
JUN TAMAYA

Debut:
GAKUSHU KENKYUSHA
"MEGAMI MAGAZINE"
SEPTEMBER 2007 ISSUE (VOL.88)

P-040

Illustration:
HIROKI SHINAGAWA

Debut:
GAINAX NET
"ALTERNATE VISIONS"
ROUND 5

P-037

Illustration:
HIROKI SHINAGAWA

Debut:
GAINAX NET
"ALTERNATE VISIONS"
ROUND 1

P-029

Base Art:
YAMATO KOJIMA

Finish: SANOKUMI

BG:
JUN TAMAYA

Debut:
GAKUSHU KENKYUSHA
"MEGAMI MAGAZINE"
DECEMBER 2007 ISSUE (VOL.91)

P-040

Illustration:
HIROKI SHINAGAWA

Debut:
GAINAX NET
"ALTERNATE VISIONS"
ROUND 6

P-037

Illustration:
HIROKI SHINAGAWA

Debut:
GAINAX NET
"ALTERNATE VISIONS"
ROUND 2

P-030

Base Art:
YOU YOSHINARI

Debut:
VOL.02 COVER

P-040

Illustration:
HIROKI SHINAGAWA

Debut:
GAINAX NET
"ALTERNATE VISIONS"
ROUND 6

P-037

Illustration:
HIROKI SHINAGAWA

Debut:
GAINAX NET
"ALTERNATE VISIONS"
ROUND 2

P-031

Base Art:
HIROAKI TOMITA

Finish: SANOKUMI

BG:
HIROAKI TOMITA

Debut:
KODANSHA "TV MAGAZINE"
AUGUST 2007 ISSUE

P-040

Illustration:
HIROKI SHINAGAWA

Debut:
GAINAX NET
"ALTERNATE VISIONS"
FINAL ROUND

P-037

Illustration:
HIROKI SHINAGAWA

Debut:
GAINAX NET
"ALTERNATE VISIONS"
ROUND 3

P-032

Base Art:
AKIRA AMEMIYA

Finish: SANOKUMI

Debut:
KODANSHA
"TV MAGAZINE"
MAY 2007 ISSUE

P-040

Illustration:
HIROKI SHINAGAWA

Debut:
GAINAX NET
"ALTERNATE VISIONS"
FINAL ROUND

P-038

Illustration:
HIROKI SHINAGAWA

Debut:
GAINAX NET
"ALTERNATE VISIONS"
ROUND 3

P-034

Base Art:
AKIRA AMEMIYA

Finish: SANOKUMI

Debut:
KODANSHA
"TV MAGAZINE"
JUNE 2007 ISSUE

P-055

Base Art:
MASAHITO ONODA
Finish: SANOKUMI
Debut:
TOKUMA SHOTEN
"MOEMAGE"
FIRST ISSUE

P-051

Illustration:
HIROKI SHINAGAWA
Debut:
KADOKAWA SHOTEN
"COMPTIQ MONTHLY"
JULY 2008 ISSUE

P-041

Base Art:
ATSUSHI NISHIGORI
Finish: SANOKUMI
SFX: ATSUSHI NISHIGORI
Debut:
ANIMATED FILM
"THE CRIMSON LOTUS
CHAPTER" MAIN VISUAL

P-056

Base Art:
ATSUSHI NISHIGORI
Finish: SANOKUMI
Debut:
ICHIJINSHA
"CHARA★MEL"
VOL.6 COVER

P-051

Illustration:
HIROKI SHINAGAWA
Debut:
KADOKAWA SHOTEN
"COMPTIQ MONTHLY"
AUGUST 2008 ISSUE

P-042

Base Art:
YOU YOSHINARI
Debut:
ANIMATED FILM
"THE CRIMSON LOTUS
CHAPTER" MAIN VISUAL

P-057

Illustration:
ATSUSHI NISHIGORI
Debut:
ICHIJINSHA
"CHARA★MEL"
VOL.6 PIN-UP

P-052

Illustration:
HIROKI SHINAGAWA
Debut:
KADOKAWA SHOTEN
"COMPTIQ MONTHLY"
SEPTEMBER 2008 ISSUE

P-043

Base Art:
ATSUSHI NISHIGORI
Finish: SANOKUMI
SFX: ATSUSHI NISHIGORI
BG: HIROKI SHINAGAWA
Debut:
ANIMATED FILM OPENING
PARTY MAIN VISUAL

P-058

Base Art:
RYOJI MASUYAMA
Finish: SANOKUMI
Debut:
GAKUSHU KENKYUSHA
"MEGAMI MAGAZINE"
NOVEMBER 2008
ISSUE (VOL.102)

P-052

Illustration:
HIROKI SHINAGAWA
Debut:
KADOKAWA SHOTEN
"COMPTIQ MONTHLY"
OCTOBER 2008 ISSUE

P-044

Base Art:
ATSUSHI NISHIGORI
Finish: SANOKUMI
Debut:
KADOKAWA SHOTEN
"NEWTYPE MONTHLY"
APRIL 2008 ISSUE

P-059

Base Art:
IKUO KUWANA
Finish:
HIROMI WAKABAYASHI
Debut:
GAKUSHU KENKYUSHA
"MEGAMI MAGAZINE"
OCTOBER 2008 ISSUE
BONUS CONTENT (VOL.101)

P-053

Illustration:
HIROKI SHINAGAWA
Debut:
KADOKAWA SHOTEN
"COMPTIQ MONTHLY"
NOVEMBER 2008 ISSUE

P-046

Base Art:
HIROYUKI IMAISHI
Finish: SANOKUMI
Debut:
KADOKAWA SHOTEN
"NEWTYPE MONTHLY"
OCTOBER 2008 ISSUE

P-059

Base Art:
IKUO KUWANA
Finish:
SANOKUMI
Debut:
GAKUSHU KENKYUSHA
"MEGAMI MAGAZINE"
OCTOBER 2008 ISSUE
BONUS CONTENT (VOL.101)

P-053

Illustration:
HIROKI SHINAGAWA
Debut:
KADOKAWA SHOTEN
"COMPTIQ MONTHLY"
DECEMBER 2008 ISSUE

P-048

Base Art:
IKUO KUWANA
Finish: SANOKUMI
SFX:
FUMIHIKO MOROHASHI
Debut:
KADOKAWA SHOTEN
"NEWTYPE MONTHLY"
NOVEMBER 2008 ISSUE

P-060

Base Art:
ATSUSHI NISHIGORI
Finish: SANOKUMI
SFX: ATSUSHI NISHIGORI
Debut:
GAKUSHU KENKYUSHA
"MEGAMI MAGAZINE"
OCTOBER 2008 ISSUE COVER
(VOL.101)

P-054

Illustration:
ATSUSHI NISHIGORI
Debut:
BIJUTSU SHUPPANSHA
"COMICKERS ART STYLE"
VOL.7 COVER

P-050

Base Art:
KOUICHI MOTOMURA
Finish: SANOKUMI
SFX:
TOYONORI YAMADA
Debut:
KADOKAWA SHOTEN
"NEWTYPE MONTHLY"
AUGUST 2008 ISSUE

P-061

Illustration:
YOU YOSHINARI
Debut:
ANIMATED FILM
"THE SPIRAL STONE CHAPTER"
MAIN VISUAL

P-055

Layout:
ATSUSHI NISHIGORI
Base Art: RYOTA HAYATSU
Finish: SANOKUMI
Debut:
TOKUMA SHOTEN
"ANIMAGE MONTHLY"
AUGUST 2008 ISSUE

P-050

Base Art:
ATSUSHI NISHIGORI
Finish: SANOKUMI
SFX:
FUMIHIKO MOROHASHI
Debut:
KADOKAWA SHOTEN
"NEWTYPE MONTHLY"
SEPTEMBER 2008 ISSUE

P-092

Illustration:
YOU YOSHINARI

Debut:
ANIPLEX TV EDITION
DVD VOLUME 8
BONUS BOX

P-094

Illustration:
KAZUHIKO SHIMAMOTO

Debut:
ANIPLEX TV EDITION
DVD VOLUME 5
BONUS DISK

P-096

Illustration:
YUSUKE YOSHIGAKI

Debut:
ANIPLEX TV EDITION
DVD VOLUME 1
BONUS DISK

P-096

Illustration:
YOU YOSHINARI

Debut:
ANIPLEX ORIGINAL
SOUNDTRACK
CD JACKET

P-096

Illustration:
YOU YOSHINARI

Debut:
ANIPLEX ORIGINAL
SOUNDTRACK
CD JACKET

P-097

Base Art: ATSUSHI NISHIGORI
Finish: SANOKUMI
SFX: ATSUSHI NISHIGORI
BG: BIHOU

Debut:
SONY MUSIC RECORDS
"SKY-BLUE DAYS"
(GURREN LAGANN DISC) CD JACKET

P-097

Base Art: ATSUSHI NISHIGORI
Finish: SANOKUMI
SFX: ATSUSHI NISHIGORI
BG: BIHOU

Debut:
SONY MUSIC RECORDS
"CONTINUING WORLD"
(GURREN LAGANN DISC) CD JACKET

P-098

Illustration:
ATSUSHI NISHIGORI

Debut:
ANIPLEX BEST SOUND
CD JACKET

P-078

Illustration:
ATSUSHI NISHIGORI

Debut:
ANIPLEX TV EDITION
DVD VOLUME 4 JACKET

P-080

Illustration:
ATSUSHI NISHIGORI

Debut:
ANIPLEX TV EDITION
DVD VOLUME 5 JACKET

P-082

Illustration:
ATSUSHI NISHIGORI

Debut:
ANIPLEX TV EDITION
DVD VOLUME 6 JACKET

P-084

Illustration:
ATSUSHI NISHIGORI

Debut:
ANIPLEX TV EDITION
DVD VOLUME 7 JACKET

P-086

Illustration:
ATSUSHI NISHIGORI

Debut:
ANIPLEX TV EDITION
DVD VOLUME 8 JACKET

P-088

Illustration:
ATSUSHI NISHIGORI

Debut:
ANIPLEX TV EDITION
DVD VOLUME 9 JACKET

P-089

Illustration:
ATSUSHI NISHIGORI

Debut:
ANIPLEX TV EDITION
DVD VOLUME 9 JACKET

P-090

Illustration:
YOU YOSHINARI

Debut:
ANIPLEX TV EDITION
DVD VOLUME 2
BONUS BOX

P-062

Base Art:
AKIRA AMEMIYA
Finish: SANOKUMI
SFX:
FUMIHIKO MOROHASHI
BG: BIHOU

KADOKAWA SHOTEN
"NEWTYPE MONTHLY"
FEBRUARY 2009 ISSUE

P-064

Base Art: SUSHIO

Finish:
SANOKUMI / SUSHIO

Debut:
KADOKAWA SHOTEN
"NEWTYPE MONTHLY"
APRIL 2009 ISSUE

P-066

Illustration:
HIROKI SHINAGAWA

Debut:
KADOKAWA SHOTEN
"COMPTIQ MONTHLY"
FEBRUARY 2009 ISSUE

P-068

Illustration:
HIROKI SHINAGAWA

Debut:
KADOKAWA SHOTEN
"COMPTIQ MONTHLY"
MARCH 2009 ISSUE

P-070

Illustration:
HIROKI SHINAGAWA

Debut:
KADOKAWA SHOTEN
"COMPTIQ MONTHLY"
APRIL 2009 ISSUE

P-072

Illustration:
ATSUSHI NISHIGORI

Debut:
ANIPLEX TV EDITION
DVD VOLUME 1 JACKET

P-074

Illustration:
ATSUSHI NISHIGORI

Debut:
ANIPLEX TV EDITION
DVD VOLUME 2 JACKET

P-076

Illustration:
ATSUSHI NISHIGORI

Debut:
ANIPLEX TV EDITION
DVD VOLUME 3 JACKET

P-107

Illustration:
SUSHIO
Debut:
MOVIC STICK POSTER

P-108

Illustration:
SUSHIO
Debut:
MOVIC STICK POSTER

P-108

Illustration:
SUSHIO
Debut:
MOVIC STICK POSTER

P-109

Illustration:
SUSHIO
Debut:
MOVIC STICK POSTER

P-109

Illustration:
SUSHIO
Debut:
MOVIC STICK POSTER

P-110

Base Art:
KAZUHIRO TAKAMURA
Finish: SANOKUMI
SFX: KAZUHIRO TAKAMURA
Debut:
COSPA YOKO BODY
PILLOW COVER

P-110

Base Art:
KAZUHIRO TAKAMURA
Finish: SANOKUMI
SFX: KAZUHIRO TAKAMURA
Debut:
COSPA YOKO BODY
PILLOW COVER

P-111

Base Art:
ATSUSHI NISHIGORI
Finish: SANOKUMI
SFX: ATSUSHI NISHIGORI
Debut:
COSPA YOKO BODY PILLOW
COVER SPACE LOOK & YOMAKO

P-103

Illustration:
SUSHIO
Debut:
MOVIC STICK POSTER

P-104

Illustration:
YUKA SHIBATA
BG: BIHOU
Debut:
MOVIC STICK POSTER

P-104

Illustration:
SUSHIO
Debut:
MOVIC STICK POSTER

P-105

Illustration:
SUSHIO
Debut:
MOVIC STICK POSTER

P-105

Illustration:
SUSHIO
Debut:
MOVIC STICK POSTER

P-106

Illustration:
SUSHIO
Debut:
MOVIC STICK POSTER

P-106

Illustration:
SUSHIO
Debut:
MOVIC STICK POSTER

P-107

Illustration:
SUSHIO
Debut:
MOVIC STICK POSTER

P-100

Base Art:
TADASHI HIRAMATSU
Finish: SANOKUMI
SFX: TADASHI HIRAMATSU
Debut:
TABLIER COMMUNICATIONS
RADIO CD "ONSEN TOPPA
GURREN LAGANN RADIO"
TOPPA 1 JACKET

P-100

Base Art:
TADASHI HIRAMATSU
Finish: SANOKUMI
SFX: TADASHI HIRAMATSU
Debut:
TABLIER COMMUNICATIONS
RADIO CD "ONSEN TOPPA
GURREN LAGANN RADIO"
TOPPA 2 JACKET

P-100

Base Art:
TADASHI HIRAMATSU
Finish: SANOKUMI
SFX: TADASHI HIRAMATSU
Debut:
TABLIER COMMUNICATIONS
RADIO CD "ONSEN TOPPA
GURREN LAGANN RADIO"
TOPPA 3 JACKET

P-100

Base Art:
YUKA SHIBATA
Finish:
SANOKUMI
Debut:
MOVIC ZIPPER
ACCESSORIES

P-101

Base Art:
SATOSHI YAMAGUCHI
Finish: JUN TAMAYA
BG: JUN TAMAYA
Debut:
MOVIC FAN

P-101

Layout:
ATSUSHI NISHIGORI
Base Art:
AKIKO NAKAMURA
Finish: SANOKUMI
Debut:
ANIPLEX CHARACTER
SONG CD JACKET

P-102

Illustration:
SUSHIO
Debut:
MOVIC STICK POSTER

P-103

Illustration:
SUSHIO
Debut:
MOVIC STICK POSTER

P-124

Illustration:
YUJI KAIDA

Debut:
KOTOBUKIYA
"TENGEN KADOU
GURREN LAGANN"
PLASTIC MODEL
PACKAGE

P-126

Illustration:
HUMBOLDT

Debut:
"TENGEN KADOU GULAPARL"
(MASS PRODUCTION / GGIMY / DARY)
PLASTIC MODEL PACKAGE

P-126

Illustration:
HIDEKI ISHIKAWA

Debut:
KOTOBUKIYA "GURREN"
PLASTIC MODEL PACKAGE

P-126

Illustration:
HIDEKI ISHIKAWA

Debut:
KOTOBUKIYA "ENKI"
PLASTIC MODEL PACKAGE

P-127

Illustration:
HIDEKI ISHIKAWA

Debut:
KOTOBUKIYA "KING KITTAN"
PLASTIC MODEL PACKAGE

P-127

Illustration:
HIDEKI ISHIKAWA

Debut:
KOTOBUKIYA "DAYAKKAISER"
PLASTIC MODEL PACKAGE

P-128

Illustration:
HIDEKI ISHIKAWA

Debut:
KOTOBUKIYA
"GURREN LAGANN"
PLASTIC MODEL PACKAGE

P-118

Base Art:
KOUICHI MOTOMURA
Finish: SANOKUMI
Debut:
KONAMI TRADING CARD

P-119

Base Art:
CHIKASHI KUBOTA
Finish: SANOKUMI
Debut:
KONAMI TRADING CARD

P-120

Base Art:
SUSHIO
Debut:
KONAMI TRADING CARD

P-121

Base Art:
HIROYUKI IMAISHI
Finish: SANOKUMI
Debut:
KONAMI TRADING CARD

P-122

Base Art: AKEMI HAYASHI
Finish: SANOKUMI
SFX: AKEMI HAYASHI
BG: BIHOU
Debut:
KONAMI UNRELEASED
ILLUSTRATION

P-122

Base Art: AKEMI HAYASHI
Finish: SANOKUMI
SFX: AKEMI HAYASHI
BG: BIHOU
Debut:
KONAMI UNRELEASED
ILLUSTRATION

P-123

Base Art: AKEMI HAYASHI
Finish: SANOKUMI
SFX: AKEMI HAYASHI
BG: BIHOU
Debut:
KONAMI UNRELEASED
ILLUSTRATION

P-123

Base Art:
YUKA SHIBATA
Finish: SANOKUMI
BG: BIHOU
Debut:
KONAMI UNRELEASED
ILLUSTRATION

P-111

Base Art:
ATSUSHI NISHIGORI
Finish: SANOKUMI
SFX: ATSUSHI NISHIGORI
Debut:
COSPA YOKO BODY PILLOW
COVER SPACE LOOK & YOMAKO

P-112

Base Art:
KAZUHIRO TAKAMURA
Finish: SANOKUMI
SFX: KAZUHIRO TAKAMURA
Debut:
COSPA NIA BODY PILLOW COVER

P-112

Base Art:
KAZUHIRO TAKAMURA
Finish: SANOKUMI
SFX: KAZUHIRO TAKAMURA
Debut:
COSPA NIA BODY PILLOW COVER

P-113

Base Art: SUSHIO
Finish: SANOKUMI / SUSHIO
SFX: TOMOHIKO KOMIYA
Debut:
KONAMI TRADING CARD

P-114

Base Art: CHIKASHI KUBOTA
Finish: SANOKUMI
Debut:
KONAMI TRADING CARD

P-115

Base Art: CHIKASHI KUBOTA
Finish: SANOKUMI
Debut:
KONAMI TRADING CARD

P-116

Base Art:
SUSHIO
Debut:
KONAMI TRADING CARD

P-117

Base Art: KIKUKO SADAKATA
Finish: SANOKUMI
Debut:
KONAMI TRADING CARD

ART WORKS
Crimson Lotus / Spiral Stone

ENGLISH EDITION CREDITS

English Translation - M. KIRIE HAYASHI
Proof Reading - MICHELLE LEE

UDON STAFF
Chief of Operations: ERIK KO
Director of Publishing: MATT MOYLAN
Senior Editor: ASH PAULSEN
Senior Producer: LONG VO
VP of Sales: JOHN SHABLESKI
Production Manager: JANICE LEUNG
Marketing Manager: JENNY MYUNG
Japanese Liaison: STEVEN CUMMINGS

JAPANESE EDITION CREDITS
special thanks

株式会社ガイナックス　株式会社アニプレックス
株式会社徳間書店　株式会社学習研究社　株式会社講談社
株式会社一迅社　株式会社ホビージャパン　株式会社美術出版社
株式会社ムービック　コナミ株式会社　株式会社壽屋
株式会社コスパ　タブリエ・コミュニケーションズ株式会社　株式会社ソニー・ミュージックレコーズ

art direction + design
上杉季明 (マッハ55号)

chief editor
榎本郁子　梶井斉

editor
三枝あすか

発行者　井上伸一郎

発行　株式会社KADOKAWA

発売　株式会社角川グループパブリッシング

TENGENTOPPA GURREN LAGANN ILLUSTRATIONS: GURREN LAGANN - Loot Crate Edition

© GAINAX, KAZUKI NAKASHIMA / Aniplex, KDE-J, TV TOKYO, DENTSU
© GAINAX, KAZUKI NAKASHIMA/Gurren Lagann-Movie Committee

Edited by KADOKAWA SHOTEN

First published in Japan in 2009 by KADOKAWA CORPORATION, Tokyo.
English translation rights arranged with KADOKAWA CORPORATION, Tokyo.
through Tuttle-Mori Agency, Inc., Tokyo.

English edition published by UDON Entertainment Corp.
118 Tower Hill Road, C1, PO Box 20008,
Richmond Hill, Ontario, L4K 0K0, Canada

www.UDONentertainment.com

Loot Crate Edition: May 2017
ISBN-13: 978-1-77294-049-7
ISBN-10: 1-77294-049-6

Printed in China